Key to Pitman 2000 Short Course

PITMAN PUBLISHING LIMITED
128 Long Acre, London WC2E 9AN

A Longman Group Company

© Pitman Publishing Limited 1986

First published in Great Britain 1986

Reprinted 1986

British Library Cataloguing in Publication Data
Key to Pitman 2000 short course.
   1. Shorthand—Pitman—Examinations, questions,
   etc.
   I. Coombs, Bryan. Pitman 2000 shorthand
   653'.4242'076   Z56.2.P5

Text set in 10/12 pt Linotron Univers.
Printed and bound in Great Britain
at The Bath Press, Avon

ISBN 0 273 02480 9

Unit 1

Progress Check 1.1

1 The pay. The ape. The bay. The bee.
2 Aid Pa and Jay each day.
3 Eat it, the tea, and pay.
4 Do put it to Pa to pay each day.
5 Be an aid and do pay.

Progress Check 1.2

Pay each department to do a page. Aid Pa and / Jay to put the date. Teach Pa and Jay to / do it. Tape page two.   (*25 words*)

Reading and Writing Practice (Unit 1)

1 Eat the peach and pay.
2 Do a page each day.
3 Pay the department to do it.
4 Put the age and the date.
5 Be an aid and teach Pa to put the date.

Dictation (Unit 1)

Pay Pa and Jay to aid each department. Teach two / to do a page each day. Date each page. Put / the date and the age of each page.   (*28 words*)

Unit 2

Progress Check 2.1

Joe bought a boat. Obey Joe and tow the boat / to the bay. Tape the jaw and the paw. Tape / the boot. Chew the peach, eat it and pay.   (*29 words*)

Progress Check 2.2

Keep calm, take the key and go to the coach. / Take the coach to the bay and go to the / boat. Talk to Joe. Joe may aim to talk to / me. (*31 words*)

Progress Check 2.3

Each company may aim to make a team and go / to the game. Joe had to take charge of the / team and take it to the game. It had to / be the large coach to take the team today. Which / company had to take a boat? (*46 words*)

Reading and Writing Practice (Unit 2)

1 Joe bought a boot company and may aim to make it pay.
2 Talk to the team and take two to the game.
3 Each department put a code of the date to be bought.
4 Which large company may cope and make a go of it today?
5 Which team had to go today? Keep calm and take charge.

Dictation (Unit 2)

1 Go to each company and talk to the team. Pay / each team to teach each department to cope. A large / auto company may cope today. A cheap auto may be / the key to a boom. (*35 words*)

2 Each company may charge to take a team to the / game. Go and talk to the team coach. Make a / code of the date of the game. Keep the key / to the code. Aim to keep to the date. (*39 words*)

Unit 3

Progress Check 3.1

Check the map. Pack a bag and pick a team / to go to the bay. Dig at the edge and / make a big ditch. Check the catch each day. (*29 words*)

3

Progress Check 3.2

Say to the team, 'Go to the zoo today. It / may be easy to catch a coach to the zoo, / so pack a bag and go. Go and see the / big ape'. (*32 words*)

Progress Check 3.3

It seems easy to get a jet and escape the / system. Joe says it may be sad to sit at / a desk and do the same task each day. Jack / says busy days may be a miss. So pick an / easy desk task, and go and do a busy task, / and choose which to do.   (*55 words*)

Reading and Writing Practice (Unit 3)

1 It is the large business which makes zips and it has a city base.
2 Ask to see all of the team together and sit and talk.
3 Altogether Mrs Kay has two empty desks and space to keep all the discs.
4 As to the gas charges, ask Joe to check; it is his mistake. It is easy to make mistakes.
5 Mrs Kay is to talk to all of us today. The speech is to be 'Business Systems' and the aim is to get all of us to talk.

Dictation (Unit 3)

1 A large company today has to make charges. A city / company adds charges to despatch. All add a tax and / pay it back to the tax department. To pay tax, / and to get the charges back may all seem easy. / Sad to say each day the city sees a large / business cease.   (*52 words*)

2 Today is the day to add the zip codes. Is / it so big a task? Ages ago each large business / had a zip code. It seems a pity it had / to take days and days to get each company to / add the code. (*43 words*)

Unit 4

Progress Check 4.1

It is an odd job to do so keep a / check. It may be easy because it took such a / big team to get the job set up. Discuss it / and keep us up to date.   (*36 words*)

Progress Check 4.2

The cost of most mistakes just becomes a statistic. Check / the causes and put a stop to some. Stock checks / may assist, so discuss at which stage to take such / steps. Master the system and the mistakes may cease.   (*39 words*)

Reading and Writing Practice (Unit 4)

1 The book suggests most of the companies owe large sums, but is it so?
2 Stack the cases all together and make the most of the space.
3 Almost all of the posters suggest it is an easy business system.
4 An exhaust assists gases to escape and aids the speed of jets.
5 Who is to assist the boss and put all the messages on the cassette?

Dictation (Unit 4)

1 Almost all the statistics which do exist seem to suggest / it is easy to get a large business to the / top, but to stay at the top it has to / be the best. Guesses on costs and mistakes on stocks / seem to be the biggest causes of upsets. At first / most companies cope but sad to say as the debts / become large some companies cease to exist.   (*67 words*)

2 The first job is to check all the large departments / and see the state of each. Check the first-aid / boxes and the access to the escape exits. Such checks / must be a success; it is all too easy to / miss a box and an exit because of speed.   (*49 words*)

Unit 5

Progress Check 5.1

Cash was used to pay the wages; today they switched / to cheques. They talked of which was the best way / and it seems they swayed all of them. Most said / 'yes'. They wished the cheques to be used. (*38 words*)

Progress Check 5.2

Yes, each item was checked and packed. We had a / choice of which way it was to go, and assumed / it was up to us, and the box was despatched / to the west. They had stated to the south and / the mistake was due to a missed message. (*48 words*)

Reading and Writing Practice (Unit 5)

1 We shall walk to the shops. By choice we shall use the bus on the way back.
2 Yesterday this business boomed and we all had the best day of the week.
3 We think we shall always occupy this site because it is the best.
4 Although some items may be missed out of this issue we shall go on.
5 We always used to despatch to the south but I think we shall, and ought, to switch this month.

Dictation (Unit 5)

1 Although this is a large company which has had much / success, we must watch costs. Much time is wasted by / some departments; stock is missed and it must be assumed / this is due to easy access. These items should be / discussed by each department this week and all this month. / We must always keep a check on excess waste. (*59 words*)

2 Mr Smith wishes to speak to all of us this / week and we think the best choice of day is / Tuesday. We shall be altogether at the top

site. The / big issue we wish to be discussed is the way / we use outside teams at times, and the wages paid / to them. It is suggested they get top wages. We / wish to say to Mr Smith such wages should be / paid to us at this company. We think it is / time to discuss the issue of basic wages. Mr Smith / may seek to sweep this issue away at the talk / and we must stick together on this.   (*107 words*)

Unit 6

Progress Check 6.1

Mrs Eve Foster voiced the views of most and moved / to take a vote on the issue of the cost / of food. She said she had faith to ask them / to vote. Food costs should be fixed and they must / face up to this fact.   (*45 words*)

Progress Check 6.2

They decided it was too tough a step and gave / way to a vote. Five of them defied the wishes / of most and voted to stay out. This was defeated. / Although divided on this issue they do make an effective / team. A devoted staff achieves and makes positive moves.   (*49 words*)

Reading and Writing Practice (Unit 6)

1 I am going to suggest we move out of the city; it would be an effective and positive way of making the largest saving.
2 This is the largest savings scheme to date and so much of its success is due to you. Thank you for all you have achieved.
3 Thank all of the staff who gave so much time to give out tea and coffee.
4 We have had difficulty setting up this business and you have to face up to the facts and above all devote some time to it.
5 They have to use several forms and checking each of them is difficult. We have to discuss how much to pay them.

Dictation (Unit 6)

Memo to: Fay Smith **From:** Joseph James
Subject: Staffing **Date:** today's

We must face up to the facts and fix a / time to discuss staffing. My view is positive; we must / move staff to save jobs. We have a tough time / facing us. Several difficulties exist today because we assumed this / company was cost effective. We have assumed too much. If / we devote a few days each month to checking out / the facts we shall achieve success. It would be best / if we get together this month to discuss ways of / achieving savings. A Tuesday would be the best day for / me.   (*91 words*)

Unit 7

Progress Check 7.1

We have to be ready to carry out the rest of / the work at the factory on Thursday. Be ready to / do a thorough job. The service road has to be / put right first and we have marked the diary. Borrow / staff if you have to for this purpose and work / on Saturday.   (*52 words*)

Progress Check 7.2

Although it is difficult this firm aims to reduce errors / and we wish to say to customers they may rest assured / of always receiving a fair service. Errors do occur / during several stages and although most do get removed it / does appear some reach customers. It would take an army / to check each item. We shall go on seeking a / remedy. (*61 words*)

Reading and Writing Practice (Unit 7)

1 The purpose of this exercise is to arrive at a satisfactory rate for our customers. They were getting a poor service.
2 Take an hour or two and have a thorough read of the rest of the story and see if your views are the same.
3 Make arrangements with them to remedy the poor work and say we are sorry it occurred.

4 We shall require you to carry out all repairs at the factory today or tomorrow.

5 Already this year we have received our fair share of work and we shall make arrangements to refer some jobs to you.

Dictation (Unit 7)

1 Memo
To: All staff   **From**: Factory Fire Officer
Subject: Safety

During the week the City Fire Officers are going to / check with us each room of our firm and the / resources we have to use should a fire occur. I / have arranged for an officer to visit each department to / advise the first-aid staff. A fire-safety exercise is / to be carried out and your department may be required / to assist.   (*62 words*)

2 Memo
To: Factory Fire Officer   **From**: Chief Fire Officer
Subject: First-aid Boxes

The officers who visited your factory during the week were / satisfied with most of the resources but several departments have / first-aid boxes which require repairing. You should make arrangements / for such repairs to be carried out by Thursday. I / have arranged for an officer to revisit and make a / thorough check. I am sorry to have to make these / remarks because your company has had a satisfactory safety visit / for several years.   (*73 words*)

Unit 8

Progress Check 8.1

The profit figures for December have dropped right across this / company. This is a great surprise, or shock, and we / must try to restore the progress we were making. The / pricing programme should be checked.   (*35 words*)

Progress Check 8.2

You may disagree but the figures were right at the / time of going to press. The views you are expressing / may destroy our image and I must stress you should / take extreme care. Describing the profits drop as staggering is / a disgrace. I express the views of the Board. (*49 words*)

Progress Check 8.3

We advertise in the press every Friday, otherwise our offers / over the year would be wasted. Such measures do have / some effect. We foresee the average costs of advertising rising / so we may use the free press. (*37 words*)

Progress Check 8.4

Our crops suffered this summer and it may take over / a year for us to recover. The weather was extreme / and other farmers suffered just as much. It may be / safer to spread the type of crops we grow. (*39 words*)

Reading and Writing Practice (Unit 8)

1 Our commercial department thinks properties are recovering and more appear to be making very satisfactory profits.
2 The larger corporations have vast resources and spread more of their risks. Their shares perform better over a period of years.
3 The weather always affects our figures for the year, but having had a better summer all should be very satisfactory.
4 We wish to express our thanks to all the workers for their success on the fresh programme.
5 It is very much safer to drive this car and I gather the first service is free of charge.

Dictation (Unit 8)

1 Dear Sir
I am writing this card to every address / I have gathered from the books of this company which / I took over a few months ago. Today this is / a much larger company because I have brought together several / firms to form a very large corporation. Because we are /

so large we are offering prices which are very much / reduced. I ask you to check the prices of other / companies and I think you may be surprised at how / much more you are being asked to pay. From December / we shall have a programme of great offers spreading through / to April. Try us and see if we measure up / to all I have said. I trust this address is / correct. Yours faithfully (*123 words*)

2   Dear Sir
From Friday of this week I am offering / the very best fresh farm food with a door-to / -door service. Most of the produce is from our farm / and our eggs are fresh each day. The larger super / stores which stock such items may have had them for / a week or more before they reach you. If you / post me the attached card I shall arrange to visit / you with a wide choice of our produce. Our prices / are very fair and of course the service is free / of charge. Yours faithfully   (*94 words*)

Unit 9

Progress Check 9.1

The owner of a newspaper never knows how much space / is going to be necessary for news coming just minutes / before setting up the paper. Many changes to the design / of each page have to be arranged. The first reference / is to the editor, the manager of the paper, who / announces which changes are to be carried out. Most news / items are correct; some are wrong.   (*66 words*)

Progress Check 9.2

Banks and insurance companies often ask for a reference. Before / one joins such companies it is necessary to write down / the names of a number of men and women who / have known you for many years. Names must never be / given before asking such persons if they can assist you / by providing a written reference. Even if you often see these men and women you must always be certain by / asking if you can use their names.   (*77 words*)

Reading and Writing Practice (Unit 9)

1 Notwithstanding the fact you have insurance you are nevertheless responsible for your own things throughout the journey.
2 Several inquiries have already been received from manufacturers and this may influence those who have responsibility for advertising.
3 The train runs through the green and brown countryside from November to January and begins again in June.
4 All who manufacture anything for us have been given the news and many have said they are more than satisfied with everything we have arranged.
5 The manager has to arrange to wine and dine the staff at New Year; anyone who is going to be away should say so.

Dictation (Unit 9)

1 Letter to the Manager, Evening News

Dear Sir,
I have been reading your newspaper for many years now / but it has never been necessary for me to write / to the owners via the manager as I am doing / today. You have just announced a price increase and I / must make a strong protest against any such move. Someone / has to do something to inform you just how your / readers view this increase. I have examined the evidence and / I am more than ever sure this is a case / of profiteering. Can you deny this? There has been no / change in your own working expenses since the November price / increase. I shall be interested to have your own views / on this issue within the next few days. Yours faithfully / (120 words)

2 Memo

To: All Staff   **From:** Manager
Subject: Overtime   **Date:** Today's

A new rota has been drawn up and can be / seen on the main notice board on Monday. It is / necessary to begin the new rota next month. The bonus / scheme which had already been agreed is to be changed / again to something much better than the company offered six / months ago. (52 words)

Unit 10

Progress Check 10.1

We live longer today and now have to learn how / to lead a full and interesting life into old age. / Walking a daily mile and eating regular meals are but / two items on a long list of things said to / prolong life. (*42 words*)

Progress Check 10.2

An analysis of the annual sales reveals a general fall / in profits. We appear to be in the middle of / a battle for world sales but rather surprisingly we have / failed to explore all possibilities. Our sales people claim the / increased prices were instrumental in the fall and although this / is a possibility I strongly believe they are reading the / figures wrongly. (*62 words*)

Progress Check 10.3

Flying today is very civilised but nevertheless is positively exhausting. / This is chiefly due to jet lag and it is / essential for any company official to rest before signing any / special papers. On arrival it is useful to try to / adjust to the local time. Plan to fulfil both social / and official arrangements but only beginning the next day. By / then the traveller feels marvellous again and can cope effectively. (*70 words*)

Reading and Writing Practice (Unit 10)

1 It will be largely up to us to analyse the annual figures of the Old Mill Company Limited as soon as possible.
2 They will only be influential in making new policies for this company if they also explore all possibilities.
3 We acknowledge it is possible to be surprisingly wrong, and thankfully our losses are low, but we will try by all means to improve.
4 Early in April we will have a full-scale review of the people we employ at all levels; this knowledge will enable us to settle any special problems.
5 It is also vital we win the battle for sales in the United States and beat off our rivals, and we will enlarge on this subject next month.

Dictation (Unit 10)

1 Letter to a customer

Dear Mr Lane

Our financial year is coming to a / close and I am writing to ask you to settle / a bill from last April. There has been some correspondence / on this subject already but I am informed there is / still a balance owing. As you are an old and / valued customer I feel there must be something wrong which / has allowed this state of affairs to be reached and / by all means possible I wish to resolve any problems. / Please inform me if you have any reason for leaving / this bill unpaid. If there are no problems please pay / the sum in full as soon as possible. Yours sincerely, / Financial Manager. (*112 words*)

2 Letter to a friend

Dear Joan

At last I have a job and life / is lovely again. It took me longer than I imagined / but I suppose I was lucky in many ways because / other people I know have been seeking work for months. / I am thankful to be earning money and the salary / is reasonable. I strongly urge you to begin looking for / a job as soon as possible, and long before you / finish your training. Unless you apply soon you will be / unemployed longer than is necessary. Remember you have to sell / yourself to the employer and by all means possible stress / the marvellous course you are taking and how invaluable you / will be as an employee. I am enclosing my new / address and telephone number. Please get in touch as soon / as you can. Sincerely (*134 words*)

Unit 11

Progress Check 11.1

A meeting was called to discuss the effects of the / budget. The recent report on exports shows all records have / been broken as a result of the amended methods we / adopted last year. The new tax laws are noted with / regret because no-one has any doubts about the bad / effects they will have. It is a pity civil servants / and those who govern adopt such a poor attitude to / the business world. Solid support is seldom received. (*78 words*)

Progress Check 11.2

He made ends meet but like thousands of others found / his standard of living was not as high as he / had hoped. He had to modernise the whole factory and / the heavy costs ran into many hundreds of pounds. However / hard he tried to reduce them heating costs were high, / even in the height of summer. The needs of the / individual business owner are many but little or no help / is available. (*72 words*)

Progress Check 11.3

I think it is necessary to talk to the staff / and in particular the new staff. I would be willing / to call a meeting immediately and if it is possible / it should be tomorrow. In order to speed things up / I will ask Tom Jackson to make the arrangements. I / hope he will be able to get most staff together / and if he can he will organise refreshments. (*68 words*)

Reading and Writing Practice (Unit 11)

1 The export results for the year were discussed immediately at the end of the annual general meeting.
2 There is no doubt that our methods of selling are highly successful in this very difficult market but we cannot afford to relax our hold.
3 Promptness in deliveries is essential and accordingly we need to modernise our system to meet the new demands and avoid delays.
4 According to my records that full load went out of here on schedule and I am unable to think of any particular reason for it being late.
5 Immediate heavy losses could run into hundreds of thousands of pounds and it would be foolish not to have the maximum insurance cover.

Dictation (Unit 11)

1 Letter to Mr H Holmes

Dear Mr Holmes,
I have great pleasure in sending you / this reference on behalf of David Hughes. According to my / records he left my employment five years ago to benefit / himself by accepting a high-level post

overseas. Throughout his / time at this firm he was prompt, accurate with his / work, always willing to assist his colleagues and he was / responsible for setting standards and obtaining a record output. He / is a proud man and he knows that he is / gifted. I regretted him leaving and in all honesty I / have been unable to replace him. I know David wants / to return to his home country immediately and it is / a great pity that I cannot offer him a job / at once. He will be found to be a first / -class employee. I hope he will be happy on his / return to England. Yours sincerely, Robert Jones, Manager. (*148 words*)

2   Memo

To: Sales Manager   **From**: Personnel Manager
Subject: Peter Adamson, Sales Staff

Peter Adamson will start work on the first of next / month. He cannot begin immediately because he has to give / his present firm four weeks' notice. I was particularly impressed / by him and I believe that he is going to / be a strong member of the team. If it is / possible please arrange to take him around yourself. However if / you cannot do so please ensure he meets everyone of / importance within the first week. I have high hopes of / this new recruit.   (*83 words*)

Unit 12

Progress Check 12.1

According to a recent article in the press a good / linguist obtains employment quite quickly and often immediately she qualifies. / The larger companies request the services of such a specialist / and quite often this involves moving to where the work / is on offer. Shorthand is a linguistic skill and this / is why those who distinguish themselves in languages are generally / good at shorthand.   (*63 words*)

Progress Check 12.2

Notwithstanding the lowest trade figures for many years in this / area we shall nevertheless, Gentlemen, invest more money and look / toward better times. You will not need to be told / just how essential this is and I will not dwell / on the point. At some time we will reap the /

benefits but I do not know exactly when it will / be. This is not the fault of anyone but we / are not able to do anything more than has been / suggested. (*81 words*)

Reading and Writing Practice (Unit 12)

1 January, February, March, April, May, June, July, August, September, October, November, December.
2 The idea of creating a special sales area for all radio and hifi goods was quickly approved because it will help trade.
3 It is correct to state, Gentlemen, that from time to time stocks have been inadequate and some customers were not given their full quota.
4 According to a recent report in the press quite large quantities of goods are damaged when in transit notwithstanding the careful packing by the manufacturers.
5 Some time ago a qualified surveyor checked the new site towards the north but I do not know what was in his report or why it has not been published.

Dictation (Unit 12)

1 **Memo to: Manufacturing Manager From: General Manager Subject: Quality Checks Date: Today's**

Please quickly set up quality checks on the new assembly / line. From time to time mistakes are made but today / a large quantity of valves have been found to be / faulty. Whatever the cause is it must be traced and / when this has been done please set out the facts / in a brief report. Quality and quantity are equally important / in this trade. If you have any ideas on improving / manufacturing techniques I would appreciate having them working as soon / as possible. (*82 words*)

2 **Letter Miss Jean Cook from the Chief Personnel Officer**

Dear Miss Cook
Thank you for your enquiry about posts / for qualified secretaries in this company. It so happens that / I have received a request today from our export department / for a bilingual secretary with French as the main language. / The post must be filled quickly and when you have / read the enclosed job details please telephone me. This is / not the usual procedure for recruiting staff because whenever

there / is a vacancy we advertise in one of the quality / newspapers. What is needed in this case however is a / rapid replacement and your enquiry is most timely. I look / forward to hearing from you within a day or two. / Yours sincerely, Jane Robinson, Chief Personnel Officer. (*117 words*)

Unit 13

Progress Check 13.1

A letter should be sent to all customers informing them / that all future orders will be handled by this centre. / After 1 May orders for delivery by the end of / the month should be received by the Friday afternoon of / the second week and any arriving later will be delayed. / All materials should be ordered by the metre and a / reminder about this matter should be enclosed with each order. / (*70 words*)

Progress Check 13.2

At least a quarter of our costs go to our / distributors, and another large percentage to the machine operators and / printers. A further increase in costs takes place in the / winter for extra heating. This gives you the general picture. / I wonder if the directors have taken these factors into / account? (*51 words*)

Reading and Writing Practice (Unit 13)

1 After Easter and until further notice we shall in fact be open in the afternoons. We shall remain open later in the summer than in the winter months.
2 A letter under my signature suggested an alternative arrangement and I understand that the deposit is a matter to be discussed later.
3 I believe there is another matter to be discussed and therefore a meeting should be arranged later in order that a full picture be obtained.
4 As a matter of fact expenditure for the first quarter was over budget and if there is no change this month some other economies must be made.
5 The directors said in their opinion that the company had a wonderful future and shareholders therefore had no need to worry.

Dictation (Unit 13)

1 Letter to Sarah James about an interview

Dear Miss James
I am pleased to inform you that / you are invited to attend for an interview on the / afternoon of 7 April. The exact time will be given / to you after you have acknowledged this letter. Please report / to the small lecture theatre in the main building of / the university. Dr Anderson will address all the applicants for / the post of Personal Assistant before seeing you individually later / in the afternoon. Dr Anderson usually dictates a short letter / to each applicant which is transcribed after the interview on / an electric typewriter in my office, and I suggest therefore / that you bring a notebook and pen with you. You / stated in your letter that a character reference had been / delayed through a misunderstanding; please bring this to the interview / if in fact you have received it by then. I / look forward to meeting you next week. Yours sincerely, Pamela / Rogers, Personal Assistant. (*153 words*)

2 Interviews

During an interview you should receive a full picture of / the job and immediately after an interview you should be / able to accept or reject a post if offered. When / called for an interview make a note on the calendar / and plan to be punctual. It there is any doubt / about how long it will take you to get there / telephone the firm for details and then allow ample time. / It is important to look your best and I think / there is much to be said for dressing formally. In / order that you may also feel relaxed however you should / choose something neither too formal nor too casual. In the / near future some other ways of selecting for jobs might / be introduced. (*122 words*)

Unit 14

Progress Check 14.1

The company receives comments concerning quality control and recognises all / of these must be considered very carefully. This company will / continue to be concerned about our customers and the community / at large. Complaints which become very common about any one /

particular product may result in such an item being discontinued. / I am confident we will continue to be leaders in / this field.   (*62 words*)

Progress Check 14.2

Customers demand a totally reliable service and it should be / unnecessary to stress that any irresponsible handling of orders may / result in a loss of future orders. Those responsible for / dealing directly with customers must always be extremely patient even / when dealing with very impatient individuals. Unfortunately a dissatisfied customer / does not always let us know the reason for leaving. /   (*60 words*)

Reading and Writing Practice (Unit 14)

1   Unfortunately most of us have to pay income tax and it is illegal for anybody to try to avoid paying by not completing an annual return.
2   Unfortunately nothing can be done that is not already being done to combat incompetence within the company.
3   The committee has a large community to control but will continue to recommend help if the circumstances demand it.
4   Anybody attending the conference should complete the form to confirm their booking and return it without any unnecessary delay.
5   Staff in control of machines must discontinue the now very common and irresponsible practice of leaving machines switched on during breaks; nothing could be more dangerous.

Dictation (Unit 14)

1   Letter to the Manager, Ace Advertising Limited

Dear Sir

Your company has been recommended to me by / several of my contacts in the clothing industry. They consider / that your complete advertising service is considerably above average and / some recognise you to be without equal. I am considering / embarking upon an advertising campaign to launch a new line / which, with the right approach, I am confident will be / a great success. All concerned in this venture wish to / contribute with ideas about how to sell to the public / so your firm will be dealing with a team rather / than an individual. In the circumstances I thought it only / fair to warn you. Anyhow, you know in advance what / to expect before you complete any contract. Please contact me at / your earliest convenience. Yours faithfully, Sally Regan, Design Manager. (*129 words*)

2 Memo to: All Staff Subject: Annual Holiday

The company will close for the complete three weeks commencing / 27 July. During this time however the contract maintenance work / will take place and it will be necessary for a / few staff to take control. I am confident that there / will be enough volunteers for this work and it will **/** be unnecessary for me to allocate staff. Fortunately we have / a number of single people who no doubt will consider / it to their advantage to take holidays outside the peak / period. I need to have the names of volunteers by / the end of this week to complete the holiday arrangements. **/** (*100 words*)

Unit 15

Progress Check 15.1

Attention is drawn to the national figures for inflation, which / compare more than favourably with the international figures available. A / solution to the inflation problem seems to have been found / and special mention must be made of the Minister responsible. / We have been given an explanation of the policy and **/** a close examination of this suggests that it is working. / (*60 words*)

Progress Check 15.2

Only in exceptional circumstances will production be allowed to drop. / If the option is to employ additional staff there will / be no objection. Our whole operation, including all quotations, is / based on an assumption of full production. On occasions there / have been instructions about modifications to machinery and these have **/** been carried out without any loss of time. (*58 words*)

Reading and Writing Practice (Unit 15)

1   Your attention is drawn to the prices of our television sets which in spite of inflation are lower than most of the national stores.

2 An examination of our latest fashion collection from international designers will be worthwhile and the prices are quite exceptional.

3 Satisfaction is guaranteed when you take one of the vocational training courses, most of which lead to a recognised qualification.

4 Additional quotations are necessary before the Automobile Association will give instructions for the repairs to be carried out.

5 Information about cheap flights across the Atlantic Ocean is available on production of proof of belonging to this organisation.

Dictation (Unit 15)

1 Letter to the Manager, Computers International

Dear Sir

My attention was drawn to your television advertising / this week and the mention of an opportunity to test / machinery in my own office without any obligation to purchase / appeals to me. I would very much like to have / a discussion with someone about the type of machine I / should purchase, with a demonstration and then the chance for / a thorough practical examination of its workings in the office / situation where it would be used. I consider this to / be an exceptional offer and it will provide essential information / for a potential purchaser. I have taken the decision to / install a word processor and I am in a position / to make a purchase just as soon as I can / be assured of satisfaction. Obviously I will have to live / with my decision for some years so the final selection / is most important. The cooperation of your organisation in this / matter will be greatly appreciated. Yours faithfully, Elizabeth Storey, Sales / Director.   (*161 words*)

2 Circular letter to all customers

Dear Customer

Your attention is called to the large discounts / and special offers this month on the price list I / am enclosing for your information. On the instructions of the / directors these exceptional prices are offered to clear stock before / moving to our new divisional headquarters. With the exception of / the special offers which have been available for some time / all prices have been reduced. Special mention must be made / of the bargains in ladies fashions and in particular the / French collection. Additional offers will be made daily. I look / forward to seeing you again soon at this address and / to welcoming you to our new location next month. Yours / sincerely, John Anderson, Manager. (*114 words*)

Unit 16

Progress Check 16.1

The department is to make an announcement about the appointment / of a new manager. Apparently there is to be a / postponement of this appointment much to the disappointment of all / who applied. Although someone is urgently needed the Directors decided / on an adjournment of the selection panel and this was / mainly if not wholly at the request of the Chairman. / An amendment to the advertisement is to be made but / certainly all those already interviewed will still be considered. (*79 words*)

Progress Check 16.2

Basically membership is open to all but the chairmanship is / strictly regulated by a special committee. The relationship between members / and this committee is very friendly. Statistically the representation of / members on this committee is very unfair but the spirit / of friendship in the Club is such that no-one / seems to object. Leadership is all important in such matters. / (*60 words*)

Reading and Writing Practice (Unit 16)

1 The appointment is made for 1500 hours on 22nd July and the interview should be completed by 1700 hours.
2 The insurance claim was for 1,600 tons of grain and the amount claimed is in excess of £9,000.
3 The Club membership is now over 950 and at weekends the clubhouse is open from 10 a.m. until 11 p.m.
4 In the first hour only four or five people attended, which was a disappointment, but by 1 o'clock between fifty and sixty had been to view.
5 An acknowledgement was sent to each of the 200 applicants and a shortlist of 10 will be drawn up by the 21st of the month.

Dictation (Unit 16)

1 Letter to the Manager, New Insurance Company Limited

Dear Sir

This letter is being sent with my claim / form in the hope that after reading it you will / appreciate how urgently I need to have this matter settled. / I am also enclosing four enlargements of photographs which clearly / illustrate the damage suffered by my vehicle.

I recently opened / a new business, on the 17th of last month to / be precise, and it was essential to have a delivery / van for which I paid £5,980. I make daily deliveries / locally and whilst on such a journey last Monday another / vehicle suddenly emerged from a side road and there was / a collision. This was at 5 p.m. when there were many / people about and I have the names of three witnesses. / Legally the other driver was totally at fault and there / will certainly be no problem proving this but apparently there / is a long delay in settling claims. I am wholly / dependent on transport and am desperately in need of an / immediate replacement of my delivery van. A settlement within 24 / hours will save my business and I request that you / give this matter your immediate attention. Yours faithfully, John Lowe. / (*190 words*)

2 Letter to Mr G R Bond, Studio Interiors, Newcastle upon Tyne

Dear Mr Bond

Thank you for dealing with my order / so promptly last week. I now urgently need 14 additional / rolls of paper, the pink one which retailed at £9.50 / a roll, the reference number for which I have lost. / I also want 20 metres of the matching material, which / was priced at approximately £12.65. I have suddenly decided to / decorate an adjoining bedroom and I want it identical. My / cheque for £50 as a deposit is enclosed and / I would be very grateful to have delivery by the / 23rd. Yours sincerely, Patricia Lee. (*95 words*)